EDGE BOOKS™

Huskies, Mastiffs, and Other

WORKING DOGS

by Tammy Gagne

CAPSTONE PRESS
a capstone imprint

Edge Books are published by Capstone Press,
1710 Roe Crest Drive, North Mankato, Minnesota 56003
www.mycapstone.com

Library of Congress Cataloging-in-Publication Data
Names: Gagne, Tammy, author.
Title: Huskies, Mastiffs, and other working dogs / by Tammy Gagne.
Description: North Mankato, Minnesota : Capstone Press, [2017] | Series: Dog
    encyclopedias | Audience: Ages 9–12. | Audience: Grades 4 to 6. | Includes
    bibliographical references and index. | Description based on print version record
    and CIP data provided by publisher; resource not viewed.
Summary: Informative text and vivid photos introduce readers to various working
    dog breeds.
Identifiers: LCCN 2015045096 (print) | LCCN 2015043104 (ebook) |
    ISBN 978-1-5157-0303-7 (library binding) | ISBN 978-1-5157-0312-9 (ebook pdf)
Subjects: LCSH: Working dogs—Juvenile literature. | Dog breeds—Juvenile literature.
Classification: LCC SF428.2 (print) | LCC SF428.2 .G34 2017 (ebook) | DDC 636.73—dc23
LC record available at http://lccn.loc.gov/2015045096

Editorial Credits
Alesha Halvorson, editor; Terri Poburka, designer; Kelly Garvin, media researcher;
Katy LaVigne, production specialist

Photo Credits
Alamy/Moviestore Collection Ltd., 16 (middle); Getty Images/Peter Dennen/Aurora, 12 (top); Newscom/Dorling Kindersley, 18 (bottom), Ron Sachs/CNP/Polaris, 22 (t); Shutterstock: AnetaPics, 7, (t), B & T Media Group, Inc., 10 (b), belu gheorghe, 16, (t), Dioniya, 26 (t), DragoNika, cover (top right), 13 (t), Elena Kutepova, 15 (t), Elisabeth Hammerschmid, cover, (bottom right), Eric Isselee, 6, (b), 7 (b), 9 (b), 17 (b), 21 (b), 24 (b), 27 (b), 28, 29, Erik Lam, 11 (b), 20 (b), f8grapher, 11(t), Fedor Sellvanov, 24 (t), Idea Studio, 23 (t), Jagodka, backcover, 13 (b), 19 (b), 23 (b), LarsTuchel, 10 (t), Liliya Kulianionak, 6, (t), Marcel Jancovic, 18 (t), Michal Ninger, 19 (t), Nata Sdobnikova, 26 (b), Nikolai Tsvetkov, cover (br), rebeccaashworth, 8 (t), Roger costa morera, 4-5, S-BELOV, cover (left), Sbolotova, 25 (t), Schubbel, 17 (t), Sergey Lavrentev, 27 (t), Susan Schmitz, 22 (b), 25 (b), Susie Prentice, 1, teekaygee, 9 (t), Vitaly Titov & Maria Sidelnikova, 14, Vivienstock, 15 (b), 16 (b), VKarlov, 20 (t), YAN WEN, 21 (t); Superstock: Flirt/Flirt, 12 (b), John Daniels/ardea.com/Panth/Pantheon, 8 (b)

Printed and bound in the United States of America.
009676F16

Table of Contents

Intelligent Companions

The American Kennel Club's (AKC) working group is made up of 30 dog breeds. These dogs were developed to perform a variety of jobs. In the past they may have guarded castles or fought alongside their owners in historic battles. Some of these dogs still work as police or military dogs, sheep herders, or sled dogs. A few breeds have even been known to perform more than one of these important jobs.

Many members of the working group are also popular as pets. These medium to large canines offer their human families love, companionship, and often a certain amount of protection as well. One of the most common traits of this group is intense loyalty to the people they love most. Dogs that are not used to assist their owners in some way often crave a purpose. Outdoor pastimes, **obedience** training, and organized activities can help fulfill this need in pets. Although these dogs share a lot of traits, each working dog breed has something unique to offer. Get ready for a close look at each one!

FUN FACT

The AKC was established in 1884 and is the largest purebred dog registry in the world today.

Akita

Appearance:

Height: 24 to 28 inches (61 to 71 centimeters)
Weight: 65 to 115 pounds (29 to 52 kilograms)

Akitas are known for their sturdy bodies and curled tails. Members of this breed have thick, heavy fur.

Personality: Akitas are sometimes bold and **aggressive** with other dogs. They love their human family members with great intensity and loyalty.

Country of Origin: Japan

Recognized by AKC: 1972

Training Notes: Akitas are intelligent but stubborn. Without training they can become even more aggressive around other animals.

Care Notes: All Akitas need regular exercise. A long, daily walk is ideal. Their coats also need regular brushing to prevent excessive shedding.

FUN FACT

Helen Keller, an American author and political activist, brought the first Akita to the United States in 1937. She discovered the breed on a trip to Japan. Keller is the first deaf and blind person to earn a Bachelor of Arts degree.

Alaskan Malamute

Appearance:
Height: 23 to 25 inches (58 to 64 cm)
Weight: 75 to 85 pounds (34 to 39 kg)

The Alaskan Malamute's double coat keeps it warm in cold climates. Its coat can be black, red, or silver, but the dog's face is always white.

Personality: Alaskan Malamutes have a strong desire to hunt and capture prey, which makes them a poor match for homes with cats or other small animals.

Breed Background: Alaskan Malamutes are commonly used as sled dogs. Their powerful bodies make them perfect for this job.

Country of Origin:
United States

Recognized by AKC: 1935

Training Notes: Alaskan Malamutes are smart and highly trainable. Housetraining can be a challenge with this breed however.

Care Notes: Alaskan Malamutes need a lot of exercise. Even though a Malamute's hair resists dirt, its coat still needs regular brushing.

FUN FACT
The Alaskan Malamute doesn't bark much. But it is vocal and will "talk" to its human family.

FAMOUS DOGS
Alaskan Malamutes appear in the movies *Eight Below* and *Snow Dogs*.

Anatolian Shepherd

Appearance:

Height: 28 to 32 inches (71 to 81 cm)
Weight: 80 to 150 pounds (36 to 68 kg)

The Anatolian Shepherd comes in eight colors and two coat lengths. Most people notice that this breed is enormous. Add the Anatolian Shepherd's strength and speed and the result is a capable guard dog.

Personality:
The breed's **temperament** is a combination of protective and affectionate.

FUN FACT

African farmers use Anatolian Shepherds to guard their livestock from cheetahs.

FAMOUS DOGS

Butch from the *Cats & Dogs* movies is an Anatolian Shepherd.

Country of Origin: Turkey

Recognized by AKC: 1996

Training Notes: Early training is a must because Anatolian Shepherds are naturally independent. A loving yet firm approach works best. When properly trained these dogs get along well with people and other animals.

Care Notes: Anatolian Shepherds shed a lot. They need regular brushing, especially in the spring. These dogs love to go for long walks.

Bernese Mountain Dog

Appearance:
Height: 23 to 28 inches (58 to 71 cm)
Weight: 70 to 115 pounds (32 to 52 kg)

The Bernese Mountain Dog's coat is black, brown-red, and white. While other Swiss mountain dogs share these colors, the Bernese is different. It is the only type with long, silky fur.

Personality: This breed has a pleasant temperament. Many Bernese Mountain Dogs love people, including kids. **Socialization** is important, especially with other animals.

Country of Origin: Switzerland

Recognized by AKC: 1937

Training Notes: Bernese Mountain Dogs are intelligent, but they can be slow learners. Positive training is key with this breed. Members of this breed can develop behavior problems, such as excessive barking, chewing, or digging if they spend too much time alone.

Care Notes: This breed loves outdoor activities, such as hiking. When properly exercised, Bernese Mountain Dogs won't misbehave as often. These dogs also need weekly grooming, including brushing.

FUN FACT

An ideal Bernese Mountain Dog has a pattern on its chest that dog enthusiasts call a Swiss cross.

Boxer

Appearance:

Height: 21 to 25 inches (53 to 64 cm)
Weight: 55 to 70 pounds (25 to 32 kg)

A boxer has a short, shiny coat that is either brindle, which is brown with streaks of another color, or **fawn** colored. The breed has an athletic build and an alert expression.

Personality: Despite its sad look, this dog is anything but gloomy. It often leaps with excitement when it is happy. Boxers need to spend time with their human family members. Dogs left alone too often can develop poor temperaments and behavior problems.

Country of Origin: Germany

Recognized by AKC: 1904

Training Notes: Early training is important to keep the Boxer's enthusiasm under control. This smart breed can be stubborn when it comes to training. The trick is making it fun.

Care Notes: Boxers need occasional grooming, including bathing. They also need a lot of exercise. Boxers living in colder climates need coats while outside. Their short hair cannot keep them warm enough.

Bullmastiff

Appearance:

Height: 24 to 27 inches (61 to 69 cm)
Weight: 100 to 130 pounds (45 to 59 kg)

Everything about the Bullmastiff is huge. From its square head to its massive body, this breed's size is its most remarkable feature.

Personality: Bullmastiff owners often call their dogs "gentle giants." The breed isn't so easygoing with intruders, however. It is known as one of the bravest guard dogs.

Country of Origin: United Kingdom

Recognized by AKC: 1934

Training Notes:

Bullmastiffs can learn commands, but they don't always want to obey them. They need owners who are willing to train them continuously.

Care Notes: Owners need to keep a towel handy. These large dogs can produce a large amount of drool. Regular brushing will keep a Bullmastiff's coat in good condition.

FUN FACT

Bullmastiffs were originally bred in England to guard large game against **poachers**.

Chinook

Appearance:
Height: 22 to 26 inches (56 to 66 cm)
Weight: 55 to 90 pounds (25 to 41 kg)

Chinooks don't look like other sled dogs. Their tawny color is warmer than the black, white, and gray of Alaskan Malamutes and Siberian Huskies. Some Chinooks also perform herding tasks or search-and-rescue work.

Personality: Owners describe the Chinook as calm, trainable, and good with children. Chinooks aim to please!

Breed Background: Arctic explorer Arthur Treadwell Walden developed the Chinook breed in the early 1900s.

Country of Origin: United States

Recognized by AKC: 2010

Training Notes: The Chinook is an athletic breed. Many of these dogs compete in **agility** or obedience. Although they are highly trainable, Chinooks respond best to positive praise.

Care Notes: Chinooks are not difficult to care for. But they do shed seasonally and require regular brushing.

FUN FACT

The name *Chinook* means "warm winter winds" in the Inuit language.

Doberman Pinscher

Appearance:
Height: 24 to 28 inches (61 to 71 cm)
Weight: 65 to 90 pounds (29 to 41 kg)

The Doberman Pinscher has a sleek, muscular body. It usually has black and tan fur. Some Dobermans can be brown, blue, or fawn with orange-red markings.

Personality: The Doberman Pinscher is active, intelligent, and loyal. It can also be described as fearless.

Breed Background: These dogs were first bred to work for the military and as guard dogs.

Country of Origin: Germany

Recognized by AKC: 1908

Training Notes: The Doberman is one of the smartest dog breeds. It can learn almost any command. This breed needs a devoted and experienced owner, though. If Dobermans aren't trained well, they can challenge their owners for control.

Care Notes: Dobermans require only occasional bathing and brushing. These short-coated dogs do not do well in the cold. When spending time outside in cold weather, they need coats.

FUN FACT
In German the word *pinscher* refers to a dog's habit of jumping on and biting its prey.

13

Dogue de Bordeaux

Appearance:

Height: 23 to 27 inches (58 to 69 cm)
Weight: 99 to 150 pounds (45 to 68 kg)

The Dogue de Bordeaux has a short, fawn-colored coat. A wrinkled face, a massive head, and a stocky body are trademarks of this breed.

Personality: This breed has a personality as big as its body. This breed may act aggressive toward other dogs. However, if owners put work into training a Dogue de Bordeaux, they will end up with a good-natured pet.

Country of Origin: France

Recognized by AKC: 2008

Training Notes: A Dogue de Bordeaux will try to get its way. It is the owner's job to train this breed before that happens. Early socialization and firm training are important.

Care Notes: The Dogue de Bordeaux drools—a lot! Owners should have drool rags handy. Their short coat is easy to care for with regular brushing.

FUN FACT

The Dogue de Bordeux is also known as the French Mastiff.

FAMOUS DOGS

The character Hooch from the film *Turner & Hooch* is a Dogue de Bordeaux. Three different dogs played the role.

Giant Schnauzer

Appearance:

Height: 23 to 28 inches (58 to 71 cm)
Weight: 65 to 90 pounds (29 to 41 kg)

The Giant Schnauzer is striking in every way. Its thick, wiry coat gives the dog a distinct look. This breed is usually black or a mixture of black and white called salt and pepper.

Personality: These smart dogs demand lots of attention. Giant Schnauzers adore their human families. They are not the best choice for households with cats or other small animals because they love to chase prey.

Country of Origin: Germany

Recognized by AKC: 1930

Training Notes: Giant Schnauzers do well with training that is firm and consistent but not overly harsh.

Care Notes: Giant Schnauzers need a lot of daily exercise. Without it they can become **destructive**. Their coats also require time and effort because it tangles easily.

FUN FACT

The Giant Schnauzer is related to the Miniature Schnauzer and the Standard Schnauzer. Each one is a separate breed however.

15

Great Dane

Appearance:

Height: 28 to 35 inches (71 to 89 cm)
Weight: 110 to 180 pounds (50 to 82 kg)

Great Danes come in a wide range of colors, including black, fawn, and white with black spots. The spotted pattern is called harlequin.

Personality: Despite their large size, Great Danes are gentle dogs. They are especially affectionate with their human family members.

Country of Origin: Germany

Recognized by AKC: 1887

Training Notes: Great Danes are willing students when it comes to training. Training should begin early in a Great Dane's life. Because this breed is strong, a Great Dane that pulls when walking on a leash may end up taking its owner for a walk instead.

Care Notes: Great Danes require only occasional bathing and brushing. Owners must feed this gigantic animal lots of food.

FUN FACT

The word *Dane* means "from Denmark." But the breed's history has no known link to that country.

FAMOUS DOGS

The cartoon character Scooby-Doo is a Great Dane.

Great Pyrenees

Appearance:

Height: 25 to 32 inches (64 to 81 cm)
Weight: 85 to 115 pounds (39 to 52 kg)

The Great Pyrenees has long, thick fur that makes it look like a polar bear. This breed is big and strong, yet dog enthusiasts describe it as graceful.

Personality: A Great Pyrenees is best known for its loving temperament. This dog is a loyal companion. It also gets along well with children and other dogs. It can even live peacefully with cats if it is exposed to them as a puppy.

Area of Origin: Pyrenees Mountains, along the borders of France and Spain

Recognized by AKC: 1933

Training Notes: The Great Pyrenees is smart but independent, so it can be difficult to train. It responds well to firm, positive training.

Care Notes: The Great Pyrenees is an active breed. Owners should be aware that they can overheat if they exercise too much in warm temperatures.

FUN FACT

Great Pyrenees fossils date back to the Bronze Age (1800–1000 BC).

Komondor

Appearance:
Height: 25 to 32 inches (64 to 81 cm)
Weight: 80 to 100 pounds (36 to 45 kg)

The Komondor's corded coat makes it look like a mop. But underneath those white dreadlocks is one strong and powerful animal. The dog's coat alone can weigh 15 pounds (7 kg)!

Personality: The Komondor is not overly affectionate. It is highly protective of its human family members, however. This breed has even been known to protect other animals in its household.

Country of Origin: Hungary

Recognized by AKC: 1937

Training Notes: This breed can be independent and stubborn, so owners should begin training a Komondor at a young age.

Care Notes: Owners should learn how to care for a Komondor's cords from an experienced breeder or groomer. These dogs need a moderate amount of playtime and exercise.

FUN FACT

The Komondor has been native to Hungary, a sheep and cattle country, for 1,000 years.

Mastiff

Appearance:
Height: 27 to 36 inches (69 to 91 cm)
Weight: 175 to 190 pounds (79 to 86 kg)

The Mastiff is an extra-large dog with a short, double coat. The fur can be one of several colors, including fawn or orange-yellow, which is called apricot.

Personality: These massive animals have surprisingly sweet temperaments. The biggest battle owners usually face is getting these large dogs off the sofa.

Country of Origin:
United Kingdom

Recognized by AKC: 1885

Training Notes: Training is important because of the breed's size. Starting early is smart because Mastiffs can be stubborn learners.

Care Notes: A Mastiff's short coat makes grooming an easy task. This large dog only needs an occasional bath and brushing.

FUN FACT
Drawings of Mastiffs on Egyptian monuments date back to 3000 BC.

Neapolitan Mastiff

Appearance:

Height: 24 to 31 inches (61 to 79 cm)
Weight: 110 to 150 pounds (50 to 68 kg)

The Neapolitan Mastiff looks similar to the Mastiff. The biggest difference is size. The Neo is slightly smaller.

Personality: This breed is strong in both body and will. Neos have been described as stubborn, lazy, and independent. Many members of the breed also have a strong dislike for other dogs.

Country of Origin: Italy

Recognized by AKC: 2004

Training Notes: The Neapolitan Mastiff needs firm guidance with training. Early socialization is necessary for this breed to become a well-mannered pet.

Care Notes: Neapolitan Mastiffs bond closely with their human families. They can suffer from **separation anxiety** if left alone too much. A Neo also needs to be brushed every other week to keep its coat looking its best.

Newfoundland

Appearance:
Height: 25 to 29 inches (64 to 74 cm)
Weight: 100 to 150 pounds (45 to 68 kg)

The Newfoundland has a heavy, double coat. The fur, which lies close to the body, naturally resists water. It comes in several colors, including black, brown, and white.

Personality: It is hard to say what Newfoundlands love more—the water or children. For this reason the breed's ideal day is spent with its human family at the lake.

Breed Background: Long ago these dogs worked with fishermen, pulling nets filled with their catches.

Country of Origin: Canada

Recognized by AKC: 1886

Training Notes: The Newfoundland needs training due to its large size. Newfies respond well to gentle, positive training.

Care Notes: The breed's only demanding trait is its need for grooming. All that fur requires combing twice per week.

FUN FACT
Newfoundlands have large lungs, which makes them good at long-distance swimming.

FAMOUS DOGS
Nana from *Peter Pan* is a Newfoundland.

Portuguese Water Dog

Appearance:

Height: 17 to 23 inches (43 to 58 cm)
Weight: 35 to 60 pounds (16 to 27 kg)

Many people mistake curly-coated Portuguese Water Dogs for Poodles. The breed comes in two coat types. Short-coated Porties have tight, dense curls. The longer coat variety is made up of loose waves.

Personality: This dog's pleasant temperament makes it a popular pet. These dogs can be shy with strangers, but they love their human families.

Breed Background: Portuguese Water Dogs have a long history of working in the water. The breed once carried messages between ships for Spanish sailors.

Country of Origin: Portugal

Recognized by AKC: 1983

Training Notes: The breed is intelligent and learns commands easily. Porties respond well to positive training.

Care Notes: The Portuguese Water Dog's coat is considered **hypoallergenic**. Its coat should be brushed weekly. These dogs are also very athletic and need a lot of exercise.

▲ FAMOUS DOGS

Two Portuguese Water Dogs have made their way to the White House. The Obama family welcomed Bo in 2009. Sunny joined him in 2013.

FUN FACT

A group of Portuguese Water Dogs once worked for the San Francisco Giants baseball team. The dogs retrieved home runs in the nearby bay.

Rottweiler

Appearance:
Height: 22 to 27 inches (56 to 69 cm)
Weight: 80 to 135 pounds (36 to 61 kg)

The Rottweiler looks like the Doberman Pinscher's big brother. Their coats are the same black and tan pattern. But the Rottie is much heavier and more powerful.

Personality: This breed can be a loving, relaxed dog with its human family. Rotties are naturally protective.

FUN FACT

The Rottweiler is a descendent of ancient Roman drover dogs. These dogs helped move livestock, such as cattle, long distances.

Country of Origin: Germany

Recognized by AKC: 1931

Training Notes: Training must begin during puppyhood. Left untrained, a Rottweiler is likely to become aggressive. These smart dogs learn quickly and easily. Still, a Rottie must understand who the leader is at all times.

Care Notes: Rottweilers need lots of activity and **stimulation**. Hiking, swimming, or organized activities, such as agility, can fulfill this need. Their coat should be brushed every other week.

Saint Bernard

Appearance:
Height: 25 to 27 inches (64 to 69 cm)
Weight: 120 to 200 pounds (54 to 91 kg)

Saint Bernards come in two coat types—short and long. Shorthaired dogs have a surprising amount of hair. The longhaired variety has even more. Both come in mixtures of red and white.

Personality: Saint Bernards can make excellent family companions. These dogs are loyal and loving. Despite their size, they are great with children.

Breed Background: The Saint Bernard is known throughout the world for its bravery. This breed has a heroic history of rescuing more than 2,000 people caught in **avalanches**.

Country of Origin: Switzerland

Recognized by AKC: 1885

Training Notes: These dogs are smart and easily trainable. Because of their large size, Saint Bernards should begin training as puppies to learn not to jump on people or steal food from the table.

Care Notes: This huge pet needs encouragement to get enough exercise. A Saint Bernard also produces a large amount of drool, so drool rags are a must-have with this dog.

FUN FACT

A Saint Bernard can smell a person buried under 20 feet (6 meters) of snow.

FAMOUS DOGS

Beethoven from the movie and cartoon series of the same name is a Saint Bernard.

Samoyed

Appearance:

Height: 19 to 24 inches (48 to 61 cm)
Weight: 35 to 65 pounds (16 to 29 kg)

The Samoyed's fluffy, white coat makes it easy to distinguish from other breeds. These dogs also look like they are smiling.

Personality: What sets this dog apart from other breeds most is its personality. Samoyeds are highly vocal. They like to bark, howl, and even seem to sing. A Sammie's singing sounds like varying pitches of prolonged howling.

Country of Origin: Russia

Recognized by AKC: 1906

Training Notes: Samoyeds need training because of their high energy level. Excited dogs can be disobedient.

Care Notes: Samoyeds do not want to be inside all the time. They love spending time outdoors, especially in the snow. Their long coats need to be brushed weekly.

FUN FACT

Samoyeds are sometimes called "Smiling Sammies."

Siberian Husky

Appearance:

Height: 20 to 24 inches (51 to 61 cm)
Weight: 35 to 60 pounds (16 to 27 kg)

At first glance Siberian Huskies look a lot like Alaskan Malamutes. Both breeds are common choices for sled dogs. But the Siberian Husky shares more physical traits with its ancestor, the wolf.

Personality: A Husky's temperament is not wild like a wolf's. Huskies adore people, including kids. They also get along well with other dogs.

Country of Origin: Russia

Recognized by AKC: 1930

Training Notes: Siberian Huskies are intelligent dogs. They respond well to positive training methods.

Care Notes: Fenced yards and leashes are musts, as Huskies are known runners. Despite their high tolerance for cold weather, these dogs should not be kept outdoors all the time. Their thick coats should be brushed every other week.

FUN FACT

Some Siberian Huskies have one blue and one brown eye.

Tibetan Mastiff

Appearance:
Height: 24 to 26 inches (61 to 66 cm)
Weight: 80 to 150 pounds (36 to 68 kg)

The Tibetan Mastiff's coat can be a mix of black, brown, blue-gray, or shades of gold. Its long, thick coat is heavier in males than females. The **ruff** around the dog's neck makes it look a bit like a lion.

Personality: Tibetan Mastiffs can be suspicious of strangers, but they are great with their human family members. These dogs are natural protectors.

Breed Background: This breed has a long history as a guard dog in its home country.

Country of Origin: Tibet

Recognized by AKC: 2007

Training Notes: Tibetan Mastiffs are independent. Because of this they need early, positive training and socialization. They also have one of the loudest, deepest barks of all dogs, so they may need training to help control barking.

Care Notes: Despite their thick coat, Tibetan Mastiffs shouldn't spend long periods of time outdoors. These dogs should be brushed every other week.

FUN FACT
Tibetan Mastiffs with tan markings above their eyes are considered special. Some people believe these dogs can see danger coming in advance.

27

Other Working Breeds

Black Russian Terrier ▶

Known for: working as military dogs
Country of Origin: Russia
Recognized by AKC: 2004

. . . .

Boerboel

Known for: working as guard dogs
Country of Origin: South Africa
Recognized by AKC: 2015

. . . .

Cane Corso

Known for: hunting wild boar
Country of Origin: Italy
Recognized by AKC: 2010

. . . .

German Pinscher ▶

Known for: hunting rats and
  later as guard dogs
Country of Origin: Germany
Recognized by AKC: 2003

. . . .

Greater Swiss Mountain Dog

Known for: driving cattle
and pulling carts
Country of Origin: Switzerland
Recognized by AKC: 1995

....

Kuvasz ▶

Known for: herding and
guarding sheep
Country of Origin: Hungary
Recognized by AKC: 1931

....

Leonburger

Known for: being farm dogs
Country of Origin: Germany
Recognized by AKC: 2010

....

Standard Schnauzer ▶

Known for: working as police dogs
during World War I (1914–1918) and
later as guard dogs
Country of Origin: Germany
Recognized by AKC: 1904

....

Glossary

aggressive (uh-GREH-siv)—strong and forceful

agility (uh-GI-luh-tee)—the ability to move fast and easily

avalanche (AV-uh-lanch)—a large mass of ice, snow, or earth that suddenly moves down the side of a mountain

destructive (di-STRUHK-tiv)—causing lots of damage

fawn (FAWN)—a light brown color

hypoallergenic (hye-poh-a-luhr-JEN-ik)—possessing a quality that reduces or eliminates allergic reactions

obedience (oh-BEE-dee-uhns)—obeying rules and commands

poacher (POH-chur)—a person who hunts illegally

ruff (RUHF)—a ring of long hair around a dog's neck

separation anxiety (sep-uh-RAY-shun ang-ZI-ih-tee)—a distressful canine condition that occurs when a dog is away from its owner

socialize (SOH-shuh-lize)—to train to get along with people and other dogs

stimulate (STIM-yuh-late)—to encourage interest or activity in a person or animal

temperament (TEM-pur-uh-muhnt)—the combination of an animal's behavior and personality; the way an animal usually acts or responds to situations shows its temperament

Read More

Gagne, Tammy. *Military Dogs.* Dogs on the Job. North Mankato, Minn.: Capstone Press, 2014.

Kramer, Eva-Maria. *Get to Know Dog Breeds: The 200 Most Popular Breeds.* Get to Know Cat, Dog, and Horse Breeds. Berkeley Heights, N.J.: Enslow Publishers, 2014.

Newman, Aline Alexander. *How to Speak Dog: A Guide to Decoding Dog Language.* Washington, D.C.: National Geographic, 2013.

Internet Sites

FactHound offers a safe, fun way to find Internet sites related to this book. All of the sites on FactHound have been researched by our staff.

Here's all you do:

Visit *www.facthound.com*

Type in this code: 9781515703037

 Check out projects, games and lots more at **www.capstonekids.com**

Index